102
School
Jokes

by Michael J. Pellowski

Watermill Press

Library of Congress Cataloging-in-Publication Data

Pellowski, Michael.
    102 school jokes / by Michael J. Pellowski.
      p.   cm.
    Summary: A collection of riddles about school, including "What do
pigs bring home from school at the end of a semester? Repork cards."
    ISBN 0-8167-2579-9 (pbk.)
    1. Education—Juvenile humor.   2. Wit and humor, Juvenile.
[1. Schools—Wit and humor. 2. Riddles.] I. Title. II. Title:
One hundred two school jokes.
PN6231.S3P44 1992
818'.5402—dc20   91-20702

Why was Mr. Math sad?

His son was a problem child.

What do pigs bring home from school at the end of the semester?

Re*pork* cards.

Why did the teacher bring crackers to her meeting?

It was a parrot-teacher conference.

What class activity does Jack Frost like best?

Snow and tell.

How can you get an "A" in art class?

Be picture perfect.

Why did the wizard get only a "B" on his essay?

The teacher took off for spelling.

What goes to class and buzzes?

A bee student.

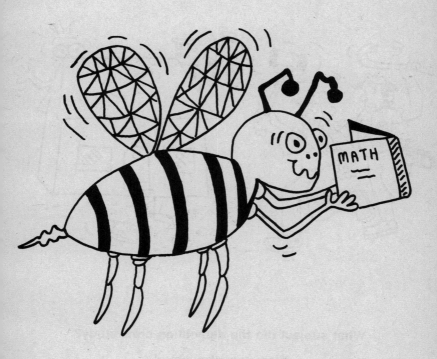

What do you call a TV set outside of a video class?

A hall monitor.

What subject did the demolition crew study?

Home *wreck*onomics!

Why did the architect become a teacher?

He wanted to draw up some lesson plans.

Why did the phone company hire a math teacher?

To check on some numbers.

What's square, has pages, and works for a newspaper?

A book reporter.

Which school subject does soda pop like best?

Fizz Ed!

What wears funny shoes, a big red nose, and carries school books?

The class clown.

What did prehistoric students carry for protection?

Book clubs.

Why did the teacher bring a dentist to school?

She was giving her class an oral exam.

What did the elephant teacher say to the elephant students?

I'm going to teach you a lesson you'll never forget.

What do hog students write with?

Pig pens.

What sound does a math clock make?

Arithmeticks!

What flies around a school at night?

The alpha-bat.

Why was the math teacher overweight?

He kept adding pounds.

How does an acrobat read a schoolbook?

He flips through the pages.

What did the cool-dude student say to the school librarian?

Yo! Check this out!

Why was the student's report card all wet?

His grades were below C-level (sea level).

Who squeaks, has big ears, and has an office in school?

The mice principal.

Why did the silly student take his report to the movies?

His teacher told him to date his paper.

Where do young trees learn their lessons?

At elm-'n'-tree school.

Why are teachers like bank robbers?

They both want everybody to raise their hands.

What kind of a pad should you bring to music class?

A note book.

Why don't teachers like to have polite students in class?

Because polite students always ask to be excused.

What science class do sheep take?

Baa-ology.

What did the fish student bring its teacher?

A crab apple.

Why was music coming from the school office?

Someone was playing the attendance records.

What did one desk say to the other?

Aisle see you later.

Why did the dentist go back to school?

To brush up on his studies.

Why is a school yard larger at recess than at any other time?

At recess there are more feet in it.

Which student wears a flea collar?

The teacher's pet.

What does a magician teacher use to grade test papers?

A magic marker.

What did the period say to the question mark?

Comma over here.

Why did the student do poorly in cooking class?

The dog kept eating her homework.

Who is the smartest pupil in the alphabet?

The A student.

Which letter of the alphabet was caught sleeping in class?

Z.

What 3 letters of the alphabet like to play hide-and-seek?

I-C-U.

Why did the student sailor raise his hand in class?

He wanted to go to the buoy's room.

Which fraction is worth twenty-five cents?

One quarter.

Why didn't the astronaut go to class?

It was launch time.

What has students, fins, and tails?

A school of fish.

What kind of fish are in the school band?

Fish that have musical scales.

Why did music play at the beginning of school?

It was time for the atten-dance.

Which class do cows like?

Moo-sic class.

Which play did the pig study in drama class?

Ham-let.

What did the calculator say to the student?

You can count on me!

Why did the judge get a bad grade in composition?

His sentences were too short.

What do band students sit on?

Musical chairs.

What do you get when a school bus has a fender bender?

Stu-dented transportation.

How does a lobster open its hall locker?

It uses a seafood combination.

Why couldn't the student become a test pilot?

His grades weren't high enough.

What has feathers and gives yearly physical exams?

A school duck-tor.

What did the gangster eraser say to the incorrect answer?

I'm going to rub you out!

When does a quarterback repeat a grade?

When he doesn't pass.

What did the pencil sharpener say to the pencil?

Don't you know it's rude to point!

Why did the builder go to school?

He wanted to learn about home additions.

What do three classroom feet equal?

A school yard.

Where did the bee graduate from?

Buzzness school.

What did one math problem say to the other problem?

I can't figure you out.

Why did the teacher take diving lessons?

He wanted to work as a sub.

What junior-high student ruled England?

King Henry of the 8th grade.

Why is a school like a kingdom?

They both have many subjects.

Why was the student snake happy?

He got an "A" in hiss-tory.

What flies and says Whom? Whom? Whom?

An owl English teacher.

What does a math teacher use to loosen a nut?

Multi*pliers.*

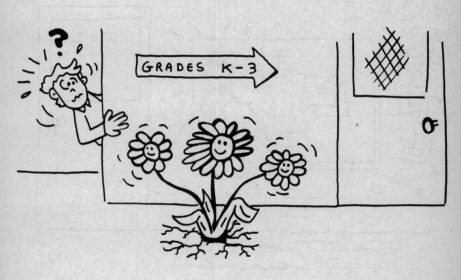

Where's the best place to grow flowers in school?

In the kinder*garden*.

Why did a bell ring when a monk walked into school?

It was time for a friar drill.

Name two classes who are brothers.

Art Class and Jim Class.

Why should you never dot another student's *i*'s?

You should always keep your *i*'s on your own paper.

What did the banker say to the test paper?

Let me give you some checks.

What bait do you use to catch a school of fish?

Bookworms.

What color should a good book be?

A good book is well *red.*

What did the Quiz Kid call his father?

Pop Quiz.

**What did the art teacher say after her class
finished reading a book?**

Draw your own conclusions.

Which chicken charged up San Juan Hill and later became President of the United States?

Theodore Roostervelt.

Who rides a dog and was a general during the Civil War?

Robert E. Flea.

What has four wheels and discovered America?

Colum-bus.

Where do you go to take a class in making ice cream?

Sundae school.

What do students of Oriental cooking do after school?

Home-wok.

Why did the window go to school?

It wanted to take a screen test.

Why did the comedian tell school jokes?

He wanted to have a class act.

What's flat, made of wood, and runs a school district?

The School Board.

Why did the cowboy point six-guns at his school books?

His teacher told him to keep his books covered.

Why was the daddy cat so happy?

His kitten brought home a *purr*fect report card.

Why was the rocket late for school?

It forgot its *launch*box and had to go back for it.

Why did the silly student carry a chair?

His teacher told him to take a seat!

What do you call a donation for the school band?

Band-aid.

Why did the witch go to night school?

She wanted to learn how to spell better.

What kind of television program did the teacher host?

A quiz show.

Why did the silly student bring a king to class?

His teacher told him he needed a ruler.

Why is a teacher like an eye doctor?

They both see a lot of pupils.

What did the student give his music teacher?

A note from home.

Why did the student bring his pet guppies to class?

Fish like to swim in schools.

What's the best way to pass a home-economics test?

Cook up some good answers.

What do you get if you cross a horn and a school instructor?

A substi-toot teacher.

Where did the railroad conductor get his diploma?

From a training school.